LEGO DC COMICS SUPER HEROES

HANDBOOK

UPDATED EDITION

SCHOLASTIC

Scholastic Children's Books
Euston House,
24 Eversholt Street,
London NW1 1DB, UK

A division of Scholastic Ltd
London ~ New York ~ Toronto ~ Sydney ~ Auckland
Mexico City ~ New Delhi ~ Hong Kong

This book was first published in the US in 2016 by Scholastic Inc.
Published in the UK by Scholastic Ltd, 2016

ISBN 978 1407 16222 5

Printed and bound in Italy

2 4 6 8 10 9 7 5 3 1

www.scholastic.co.uk

TABLE OF CONTENTS

The DC Universe features some of the most famous and incredible super heroes and super-villains ever created. Now these amazing fighters for justice and their archenemies have become LEGO® minifigures. In this book, we'll take a look at the heroes and villains, as well as their unique histories, vehicles and locations. You may even discover some secrets about the characters themselves!

CHAPTER 1
SUPER

HEROES!

IT DOESN'T MATTER IF THEY ARE AN ALIEN, AN AMAZON PRINCESS, THE KING OF THE SEVEN SEAS OR THE WORLD'S GREATEST DETECTIVE, THE WORLD RELIES ON THEM TO KEEP IT SAFE. NO MATTER WHAT THE DANGER, THEY ARE THERE, FIGHTING THE WORLD'S DEADLIEST VILLAINS. ALONE OR TOGETHER, THEY ARE THE MOST POWERFUL FORCES FOR GOOD THAT EARTH HAS EVER SEEN.

SUPERMAN

Superman is the most powerful super hero in the universe. He is a champion of truth and justice, and uses his mighty powers only in the cause of good. He makes his home in the city of **Metropolis**, but fights menaces anywhere in the world and even in outer space.

Born on the planet **Krypton**, the baby who would grow up to be Superman was sent to Earth in a rocket by his parents just before his homeworld exploded. Arriving on Earth, he was found and adopted by a kindly couple, the **Kents**. They named him **Clark Kent** and taught him to use his powers for the cause of justice.

EARTH NAME:
CLARK KENT

KRYPTONIAN NAME:
KAL-EL

WEAKNESS:
KRYPTONITE

SUPERMAN

Superman has many powers. He gets much of his strength from the rays of Earth's yellow sun, and loses his powers under a red sun.

When Krypton exploded, the fragments of the planet became a radioactive element called **Kryptonite**. The radiation from Kryptonite can cause great harm to Superman. Villains (like **Lex Luthor**) have often used Kryptonite against the Man of Steel. Superman is also vulnerable to magic.

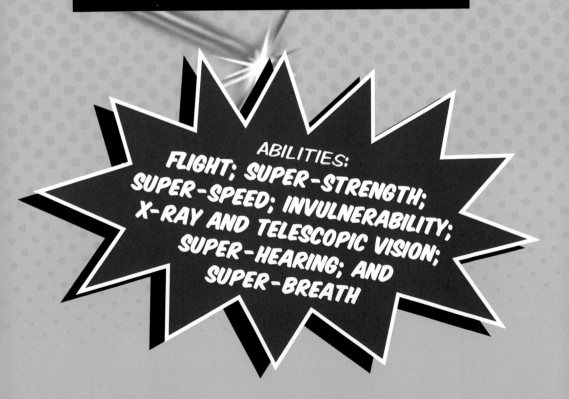

ABILITIES:
FLIGHT; SUPER-STRENGTH; SUPER-SPEED; INVULNERABILITY; X-RAY AND TELESCOPIC VISION; SUPER-HEARING; AND SUPER-BREATH

BATMAN

Batman made a lifelong vow to fight for law and order, and to stop all criminals. Although he has no special powers like Superman or The Flash, he uses his fighting skills and his brain to defeat some of the worst villains in the DC Universe.

His secret identity is **Bruce Wayne**, the richest man in Gotham City. Only a few people know that beneath Wayne Manor is the amazing **Batcave**, Batman's headquarters. When danger threatens, Bruce Wayne puts on the cape and cowl of the Dark Knight and rushes to the rescue.

BATMAN

DARK KNIGHT

ARCTIC BATMAN

SCUBA BATMAN

BATMAN

Since he has no superpowers, Batman relies on **gadgets** to help him fight crime. He has many vehicles, including the Batmobile, the Batwing, the Batcycle and the Batboat. He carries weapons with him, like the Batarang. Batman also wears special uniforms at times, like the white thermal uniform that he uses when he battles Mr. Freeze.

Batman's crime-fighting partner is Robin, but Batman often teams up with Superman, Wonder Woman, The Flash and other heroes. They are always amazed by all he is able to accomplish **without superpowers**. No matter the challenge, Batman will find a way to keep **Gotham City** safe.

ROBIN

Batman's partner, Robin, is a young crime fighter who also solves cases on his own. He combines **computer genius** with **martial arts** training he received from Batman, resulting in a double threat to the criminals of Gotham City. Robin is a master of many weapons.

REAL NAME:
TIM DRAKE

EQUIPMENT:
KENDO STICK; GRAPNEL GUN

NIGHTWING

Dick Grayson was the original **Robin**, trained by Batman to be his crime-fighting partner. When Dick became an adult, he gave up his identity as Robin to become Nightwing. Second only to Batman as a detective and a fighter, Nightwing has served as the leader for two super hero teams, the **Teen Titans** and the **Outsiders**.

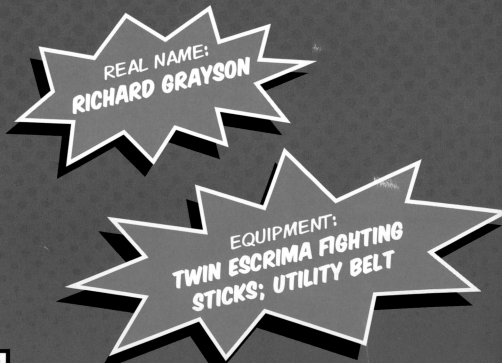

REAL NAME:
RICHARD GRAYSON

EQUIPMENT:
TWIN ESCRIMA FIGHTING
STICKS; UTILITY BELT

WONDER WOMAN

Princess Diana of the **Amazons** is on a mission to promote peace and understanding between all peoples. Unfortunately, the world is full of villains and Diana, as Wonder Woman, has to fight to protect the innocent. With **super-strength** and **super-speed**, she is only surpassed by Superman for sheer power. She also carries a **Golden Lasso of Truth**, which makes anyone caught in it answer any question truthfully.

REAL NAME:
PRINCESS DIANA OF THEMYSCIRA (ALSO GOES BY DIANA PRINCE)

EQUIPMENT:
BULLETPROOF BRACELETS; GOLDEN LASSO OF TRUTH

AQUAMAN

King of **Atlantis** and master of the Seven Seas, Aquaman is able to **breathe underwater** and **command sea life** by transmitting his thoughts to them. He can swim as fast as 100 miles per hour. He has **super-strength** and great endurance, along with enormous knowledge about the ocean and everything that lives in it.

ATLANTEAN NAME: **ORIN**

HUMAN NAME: **ARTHUR CURRY**

EQUIPMENT: **TRIDENT**

THE FLASH

The Flash can run at close to the **speed of light**, pass through solid objects, race up the sides of buildings, and even **phase into other dimensions**. He can subdue villains in hundreds of different ways, from running around them so fast that he creates a vacuum to sending them hurtling up to the sky with a mini-tornado.

REAL NAME:
BARRY ALLEN

EQUIPMENT:
THE FLASH DOESN'T NEED ANY SPECIAL TOOLS, BUT WHEN HE IS BARRY ALLEN HE WEARS A RING THAT CONTAINS HIS COSTUME!

GREEN LANTERN

Green Lantern Hal Jordan is a member of a huge organization of heroes from countless worlds throughout the universe. He gains his superpowers from a **green power ring**. Jordan quickly discovered that his ring enabled him to **fly** and to create anything he imagined out of **green energy**, from a shield against bullets to a giant hammer. The ring needs to be recharged every twenty-four hours.

REAL NAME:
HAL JORDAN

ABILITIES:
THOUGH HIS GREEN LANTERN RING GIVES HIM GREAT POWERS, IT ONLY WORKS BECAUSE OF HIS WILLPOWER.

GREEN ARROW

Wealthy Oliver Queen was stranded on a remote island. While he was there, he taught himself archery in order to survive. When he returned to **Star City**, he took on the identity of Green Arrow to fight crime. Green Arrow uses lots of trick arrows, such as a **boxing glove arrow**, a **glue arrow**, and a **net arrow** to stop crooks.

REAL NAME:
OLIVER QUEEN

EQUIPMENT:
BOW; ASSORTMENT OF TRICK ARROWS

MARTIAN MANHUNTER

Brought to Earth from his native planet Mars by accident, Martian Manhunter eventually found a home with the **Justice League.** With his powers, technological know-how and great **wisdom**, he has been an asset to the team in many ways. When not fighting crime as a super hero, he does it in his secret identity of police detective **John Jones.**

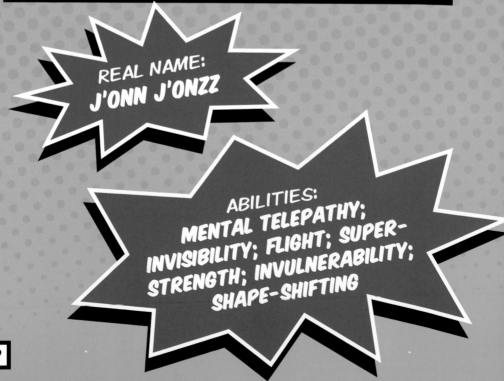

REAL NAME:
J'ONN J'ONZZ

ABILITIES:
MENTAL TELEPATHY;
INVISIBILITY; FLIGHT; SUPER-
STRENGTH; INVULNERABILITY;
SHAPE-SHIFTING

HAWKMAN

Hawkman is a winged adventurer who has lived many lives, dating all the way back to ancient Egypt. Using **Thanagarian Nth Metal**, which can defy gravity, his wings enable him to fly with impressive **speed** and **manoeuvrability**. Hawkman has been a member of the Justice Society and Justice League and frequently fights alongside **Hawkgirl**.

REAL NAME:
CARTER HALL

EQUIPMENT:
NTH METAL ON BOOTS AND WING HARNESS; MACE, AND OTHER ANCIENT WEAPONS

SUPERGIRL

Superman's cousin, **Kara**, was sent from **Krypton** on a mission to find him on Earth. An accident along the way trapped her in **suspended animation** and it was decades before she landed in Gotham Harbour. Supergirl has proven to be a valuable ally in battles against villains like Brainiac, Darkseid and Lex Luthor.

REAL NAME:
KARA ZOR-EL

ABILITIES:
FLIGHT; INVULNERABILITY;
SUPER-STRENGTH;
SUPER-SPEED; X-RAY AND
HEAT VISION

CYBORG

Badly injured in an accident, **Victor Stone** was transformed by his father into the half-man, half-machine being called Cyborg. Although at first he hated his new appearance, Cyborg eventually found new friends who accepted him with the **Teen Titans**. Later, he joined the Justice League. In addition to his powers, Cyborg is a **scientific genius.**

REAL NAME:
VICTOR STONE

ABILITIES:
ENHANCED STRENGTH, ENDURANCE, AND VISION; ABLE TO INTERFACE WITH ANY COMPUTER

BATGIRL

The daughter of **Gotham City's** Commissioner Gordon, **Barbara Gordon** always dreamed of becoming Batman's partner. After helping to save Bruce Wayne from **kidnappers**, she decided to make a career out of being Batgirl. She has helped Batman and Robin on many occasions, and also teamed up with Superman and Supergirl in the past.

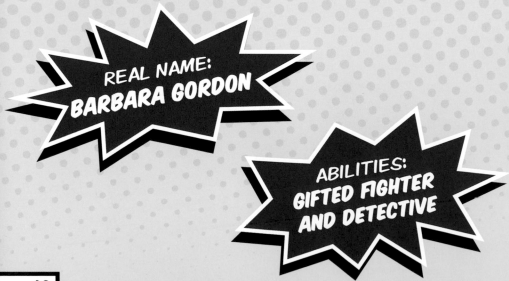

REAL NAME:
BARBARA GORDON

ABILITIES:
GIFTED FIGHTER AND DETECTIVE

PLASTIC MAN

Eel O'Brian was a small-time crook. During a robbery, he fell into a vat of strange **chemicals**. They affected the atoms of his body, enabling him to **stretch** himself at will. He decided to become a hero and named himself Plastic Man. He is a valued member of the Justice League, though his wild sense of **humour** drives some other members crazy.

REAL NAME:
EEL O'BRIAN

ABILITIES:
ABLE TO STRETCH HIS BODY INTO ANY SHAPE IMAGINABLE

LOIS LANE

ABILITIES:
COURAGE TO REPORT THE
WHOLE STORY — NO MATTER
THE DANGER

Lois Lane is a **reporter** for the *Daily Planet*, the largest newspaper in the city of **Metropolis**. Lane is dedicated to her job and incredibly brave, to the point of being reckless at times. More than once, she has found herself in danger while pursuing a story, only to be saved by Superman. At the same time, information she has dug up has often **helped Superman** solve mysteries.

COMMISSIONER GORDON

James Gordon is the commissioner of police in **Gotham City**. He was the first important city official to work with Batman and trust the masked hero. Thanks to Gordon, Batman became a valuable ally of the police. **Honest, smart** and **loyal**, Gordon is Batman's best friend on the police force. Together, they fight to keep the people of Gotham City safe from crime.

EQUIPMENT:
GUN; WALKIE-TALKIE;
HANDCUFFS

BIZARRO

Bizarro is a strange clone of Superman, created by Lex Luthor using a **Duplicator Ray**. Although he has many of Superman's **powers**, Bizarro is not very bright and tends to do everything in a backwards way. Although he wants to be a hero, Bizarro's efforts tend to do more harm than good.

BATZARRO

Bizarro used the Duplicator Ray to make clones of the Justice League. Batzarro, an imperfect double of Batman, calls himself the **"World's Worst Detective"**. Batzarro thinks a crisis is the best time to take a **nap**, that the best plan is no plan, and couldn't figure out a mystery even if the answer was right in front of him.

GUARDS

Guards are supposed to **protect** valuable places, like banks, from criminals. Unfortunately, their training doesn't cover super-villains like Two-Face and the Joker. They do their **best**, but they usually need help from the super heroes to save the day.

EQUIPMENT:
WALKIE-TALKIES;
HANDCUFFS

CHAPTER 2
VILLAINS!

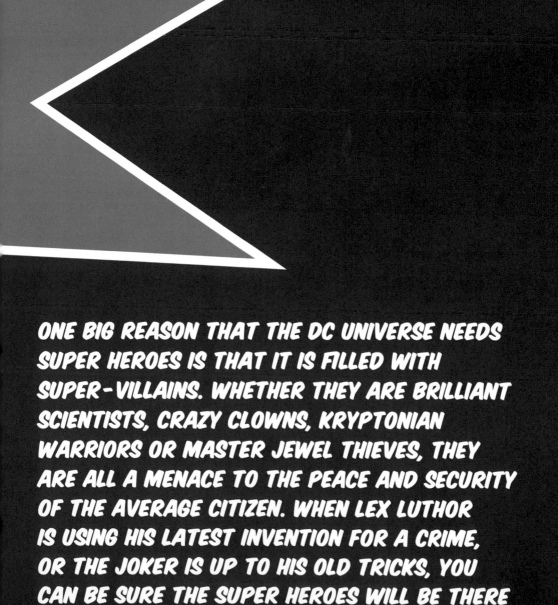

ONE BIG REASON THAT THE DC UNIVERSE NEEDS SUPER HEROES IS THAT IT IS FILLED WITH SUPER-VILLAINS. WHETHER THEY ARE BRILLIANT SCIENTISTS, CRAZY CLOWNS, KRYPTONIAN WARRIORS OR MASTER JEWEL THIEVES, THEY ARE ALL A MENACE TO THE PEACE AND SECURITY OF THE AVERAGE CITIZEN. WHEN LEX LUTHOR IS USING HIS LATEST INVENTION FOR A CRIME, OR THE JOKER IS UP TO HIS OLD TRICKS, YOU CAN BE SURE THE SUPER HEROES WILL BE THERE TO SHUT THEM DOWN.

LEX LUTHOR

The richest and most powerful man in Metropolis, Luthor knows that only Superman can stop his crooked schemes. He tries everything to defeat the Man of Steel, only to fail again and again. But with his **vast fortune** and **criminal genius**, he never runs out of new inventions to use against the Last Son of Krypton!

EQUIPMENT:
KRYPTONITE GUN;
POWER ARMOUR; LOTS
AND LOTS OF MONEY!

THE JOKER

The Joker's crimes almost always involve jokes (usually bad ones) and his dangerous **Joker toxin**. Batman always spoils his plans and they have become archenemies over the years. Sometimes it seems that the Joker commits crimes just so he can fight with Batman again. When he is not on the loose in Gotham City, the Joker spends his time locked up at **Arkham Asylum**.

REAL NAME:
UNKNOWN

EQUIPMENT:
**"BANG" FLAG SPEAR GUN;
ELECTRIC JOY BUZZER;
JOKER TOXIN**

HARLEY QUINN

Harleen Quinzel was once the Joker's doctor at **Arkham Asylum**. The Joker told her lies about himself, and she fell in love with him. After helping him escape from the asylum, she put on a costume and became his **sidekick**, Harley Quinn. She is a great acrobat and a skilled burglar.

REAL NAME:
DR. HARLEEN QUINZEL

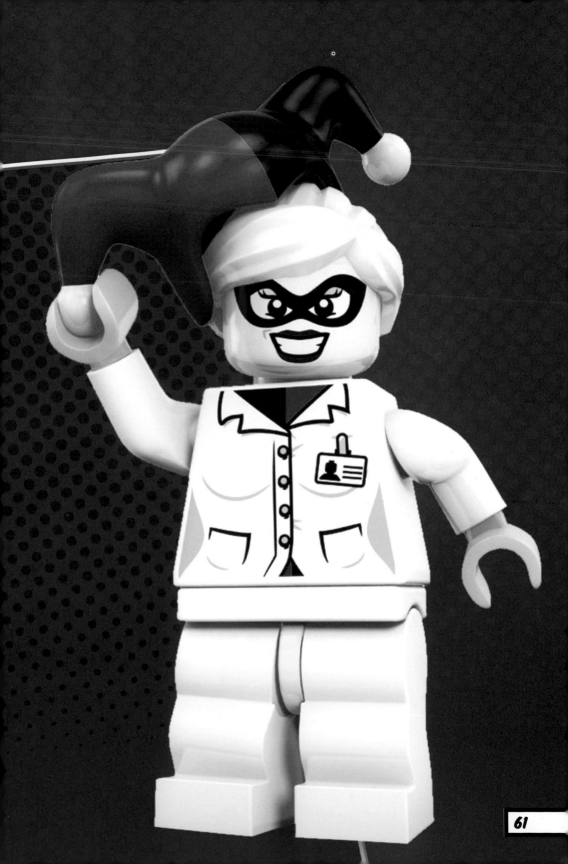

BANE

Bane is a criminal who wants to take over Gotham City's underworld. Knowing that the people of **Gotham City** look up to Batman, he decides that he must first defeat the Dark Knight to prove his power. To do this, Bane has tried attacking Batman on his own and teamed up with other villains. Although he has given Batman many hard fights, the Dark Knight always wins in the end.

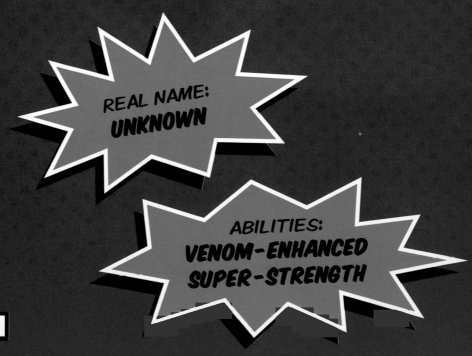

REAL NAME:
UNKNOWN

ABILITIES:
VENOM-ENHANCED
SUPER-STRENGTH

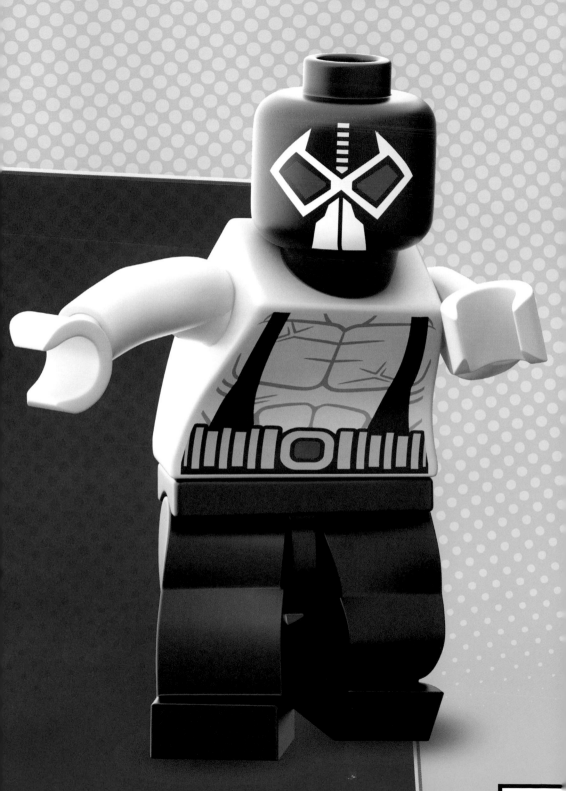

CATWOMAN

Catwoman is a highly skilled thief. Her acrobatics and **martial arts skills** have always made her a challenge for Batman. Although they are often on opposite sides of the law, Catwoman has **helped** Batman more than once when **Gotham City** was in danger. In return, Batman has sometimes let her "escape" rather than turn her over to the police.

REAL NAME:
SELINA KYLE

EQUIPMENT:
WHIP; CAT CLAWS

TWO-FACE

Harvey Dent was **Gotham City's** district attorney. Then a terrible accident resulted in half his face being scarred. Calling himself Two-Face, he became a crook, basing all of his crimes on the **number two**. Before each crime, Two-Face flips his two-headed coin, one side of which is **scarred**. He uses the coin to make all his important decisions, which makes him **unpredictable**.

REAL NAME:
HARVEY DENT

EQUIPMENT:
GUNS; TWO-HEADED COIN

POISON IVY

Pamela Isley was an expert on flowers and other plants before a freak accident in her lab turned her into Poison Ivy. Now she can **control plants**, **poison** others with her kiss, and even create new creatures that are half-human, half-tree. Poison Ivy uses robbery and blackmail to make money. Although she is not skilled in battle, she is clever, cunning and very good at setting **traps** for the heroes.

REAL NAME:
PAMELA ISLEY

ABILITIES:
CAPABLE OF CONTROLLING MANY TYPES OF PLANTS

THE RIDDLER

The Riddler loves puzzles. He uses his skill at coming up with **riddles** to challenge Batman and the police. Before every crime, the Riddler leaves a riddle clue for Batman. In fact, he can't commit a robbery without giving Batman a **clue** first! Although he usually works alone, the Riddler has teamed up with the Joker in the past and sometimes has a gang of his own.

REAL NAME:
EDWARD NIGMA

EQUIPMENT:
CROWBAR; SOMETIMES USES WEAPONS IN THE SHAPE OF QUESTION MARKS

SCARECROW

The Scarecrow uses a **fear toxin** he invented to frighten people just for fun! In his many fights with Batman, he has tried again and again to scare the Dark Knight into defeat. But Batman is smart enough to know that there is nothing to be afraid of, and brave enough not to let the Scarecrow win.

REAL NAME:
JONATHAN CRANE

EQUIPMENT:
FEAR TOXIN

MR. FREEZE

The man who became the icy villain Mr. Freeze was once a scientist studying the use of extreme cold to preserve people until the cures for their illnesses could be found. A lab accident changed him so that he could only exist in **sub-zero temperatures**. Wearing **armour** that both increases his strength and keeps him ice-cold, Mr. Freeze commits **jewel thefts** to fund his research.

REAL NAME:
VICTOR FRIES

EQUIPMENT:
FREEZE GUN

THE PENGUIN

The Penguin is a master criminal whose crimes always have something to do with birds. His favourite weapon is the **umbrella**, and he has hundreds of different kinds. These include umbrellas that allow him to **fly**, umbrellas that **shoot fire** or **poison gas**, and even **bulletproof** umbrellas he can use as a shield.

REAL NAME:
OSWALD COBBLEPOT

EQUIPMENT:
A VARIETY OF TRICK UMBRELLAS

BLACK MANTA

Black Manta is a human villain who has made a career as an undersea raider. With his powerful **Black Manta ship**, he has clashed repeatedly with Aquaman. Black Manta specializes in **smuggling** and **robbery** and has teamed up with other villains on more than one occasion. He relies on special weaponry to fight off heroes.

REAL NAME:
UNREVEALED

SINESTRO

Sinestro comes from the planet **Korugar** and was once a Green Lantern. **The Guardians of the Universe** expelled him for trying to take over his world. Now he is the sworn enemy of all Green Lanterns, but especially Hal Jordan of Earth. Sinestro's **yellow power ring** is fuelled by fear. It can create anything he imagines and also protects him from harm.

REAL NAME:
THAAL SINESTRO

ABILITIES:
YELLOW POWER RING FUELLED BY FEAR

GORILLA GRODD

Grodd is a **super-intelligent** gorilla and a long-time enemy of The Flash. Having escaped numerous times from jail cells in the mysterious Gorilla City, Grodd is on a quest to take over the world. He believes that apes should rule the planet and he won't quit until he is Emperor Grodd. And this **super-strong** scientific genius just might succeed!

ABILITIES:
SUPER-INTELLIGENCE;
MIND CONTROL

DARKSEID

Darkseid is the **ultra-powerful** ruler of the planet **Apokolips**. His goal is the complete domination of every thinking being in the universe. This has brought him into conflict with many individual heroes, as well as the Justice League. Darkseid is often the power behind the scenes of other villain organizations, as he waits for the perfect time to strike.

REAL NAME:
UXAS

ABILITIES:
DISINTEGRATOR EYEBEAMS;
SUPER-STRENGTH;
IMMORTALITY; INVULNERABILITY;
SUPER-INTELLECT

BRAINIAC

Former Scientist Prime on the planet Colu, Vril Dox's **computer-like** mind is capable of taking over other bodies. As Brainiac, he has clashed with Superman on many occasions. No matter how many times he is defeated, he is always able to re-create himself and return. Brainiac is the master of amazing **technologies** and can always be expected to do the unexpected.

REAL NAME:
VRIL DOX

ABILITIES:
GENIUS-LEVEL INTELLIGENCE;
CAPABLE OF TRANSFERRING HIS
MIND FROM BODY TO BODY

CAPTAIN COLD

Leonard Snart invented his cold gun by accident. Calling himself Captain Cold, he used his icy weapon to rob banks and jewellery stores. He can create **sheets of ice** on the ground, thick **ice walls**, or **freeze** vault doors until they shatter at a touch. Captain Cold was one of the first villains The Flash ever fought. He is still one of the Scarlet Speedster's slipperiest foes.

REAL NAME:
LEONARD SNART

EQUIPMENT:
COLD GUN

GIGANTA

Dr. Doris Zuel saved herself from a rare disease by transferring her mind into the body of a circus performer named Giganta. This gave her the power to **grow** to the size of a skyscraper and gain enormous strength in the process. Although she is a brilliant scientist, Giganta usually just smashes anything that gets in her way.

REAL NAME:
DORIS ZUEL

ABILITIES:
ABLE TO GROW TO SEVERAL HUNDRED FEET TALL; SUPERHUMAN STRENGTH AND DURABILITY

CHEETAH

Barbara Minerva is an **archaeologist** who discovered an ancient ritual that would merge the spirits of a human and a cheetah. She uses her **catlike agility** and **speed** to commit crimes, but Wonder Woman always stops her. The Cheetah has battled the amazing Amazon many times. She never wins, but is always 5ready for another fight.

REAL NAME:
BARBARA MINERVA

EQUIPMENT:
CLAWS

MAN-BAT

Dr. Kirk Langstrom tried to cure his growing deafness by creating a serum based on bats' sonar abilities. When he tested the serum on himself, he was transformed into a man-sized bat. **Wild** and **uncontrollable**, Man-Bat is a menace in the skies above Gotham City. Batman wants to cure Man-Bat – but has to catch him first!

REAL NAME:
KIRK LANGSTROM

ABILITIES:
ABLE TO TRANSFORM INTO A MAN-SIZED BAT WITH WINGS, CLAWS AND NATURAL SONAR

HENCHMEN

Most super-villains have henchmen. They **help** with the heavy lifting during crimes, **guard the hideout** and do other jobs someone like the Joker or the Penguin can't be bothered with. Henchmen tend to not be very bright, but there are usually a lot of them and they can keep a super hero **busy** for maybe a couple of minutes in a fight.

EQUIPMENT:
CROWBARS,
WALKIE-TALKIES

A SUPER HERO CANNOT STOP A CRIME UNLESS HE CAN GET TO IT IN TIME, AND A SUPER-VILLAIN CANNOT HOPE TO MAKE A GETAWAY IF HE DOESN'T HAVE SOME WAY TO GET FROM PLACE TO PLACE. OUR FAVOURITE HEROES AND VILLAINS HAVE ALL KINDS OF AWESOME RIDES — INCLUDING CARS, BOATS, PLANES AND EVEN SPACECRAFT!

CHAPTER 3
VEHICLES!

THE BATMOBILE

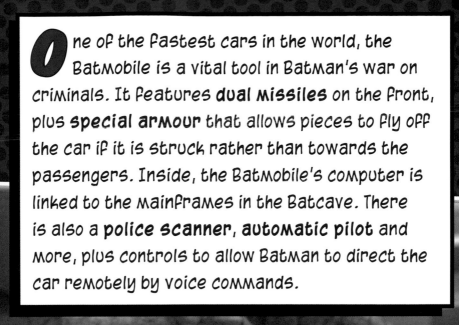

One of the fastest cars in the world, the Batmobile is a vital tool in Batman's war on criminals. It features **dual missiles** on the front, plus **special armour** that allows pieces to fly off the car if it is struck rather than towards the passengers. Inside, the Batmobile's computer is linked to the mainframes in the Batcave. There is also a **police scanner, automatic pilot** and more, plus controls to allow Batman to direct the car remotely by voice commands.

THE BATWING

Sometimes, the fight against crime means Batman has to take to the air. The Batwing is the latest in a long line of aircraft Batman has used to battle Gotham City's villains. In addition to being incredibly fast and manoeuvrable, the Batwing is armed with **twin air-to-air missiles** and is completely invisible to radar. Its engine is specially designed to make almost **no noise**, so flying villains won't know the Dark Knight is coming for them.

THE BAT SUB

When crime happens beneath the sea, Batman is ready with the Bat sub. Designed to function at extreme depths, the submarine has everything Batman needs to battle underwater menaces. Its **propulsion system** makes it one of the fastest vehicles underwater and **its twin missiles** can smash undersea obstacles with ease.

DARKSEID'S SHIP

Built by the craftsmen of Apokolips, Darkseid's ship is designed to survive the passages in between different dimensions, called "**Boom Tubes**". The massive craft is equipped with powerful **energy tentacles** capable of snatching a super hero out of the air and hurling him a great distance. The ship's **laser cannons** pack a punch and several inches of armour make the ship extremely tough to damage.

POWER ARMOUR

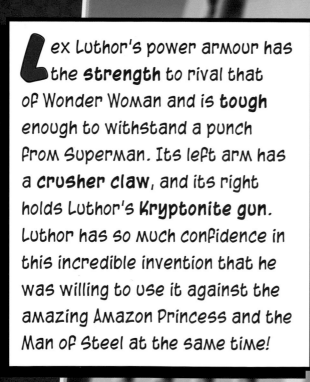

Lex Luthor's power armour has the **strength** to rival that of Wonder Woman and is **tough** enough to withstand a punch from Superman. Its left arm has a **crusher claw**, and its right holds Luthor's **Kryptonite gun**. Luthor has so much confidence in this incredible invention that he was willing to use it against the amazing Amazon Princess and the Man of Steel at the same time!

THE REDBIRD CYCLE

On missions where he needs to fly solo, Robin relies on the Redbird Cycle. The Redbird combines a **superpowered** engine with a street-bike design that allows this bird to **swoop down** on criminals, keeping the streets of Gotham City safe while Batman is away.

BLACK MANTA'S SEA SAUCER

Black Manta's high-tech ship is designed for both speed and stealth. It manages to combine **striking power** with a sleek frame that allows it to jet away after a crime is committed. The citizens of **Atlantis** have learned to fear the sight of the Sea Saucer. Even Aquaman has had problems catching up to the elusive Black Manta when he is piloting this craft!

BRAINIAC'S SKULL SHIP

The sight of Brainiac's ship in the sky is enough to send most planets' populations into a panic. With its **skull-shaped body** and **tentacles**, it looks like a monster more than a spacecraft. Armed with **cannons** and **missiles**, and packed full of alien technology, the Skull Ship has fought even the mighty Superman to a draw.

THE PENGUIN MOBILE

This one-wheeler is the Penguin's passport to a quick getaway. Armed with **twin rocket launchers**, it's narrow enough to get through alleyways where the Batmobile can't follow and powerful enough to **blast** its way through any barrier. This duck packs a punch!

THE JAVELIN

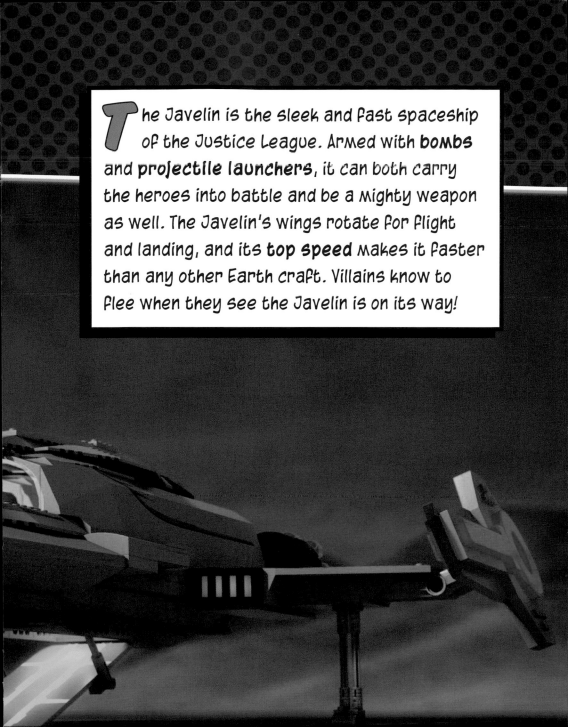

The Javelin is the sleek and fast spaceship of the Justice League. Armed with **bombs** and **projectile launchers**, it can both carry the heroes into battle and be a mighty weapon as well. The Javelin's wings rotate for flight and landing, and its **top speed** makes it faster than any other Earth craft. Villains know to flee when they see the Javelin is on its way!

THE JOKER'S STEAMROLLER

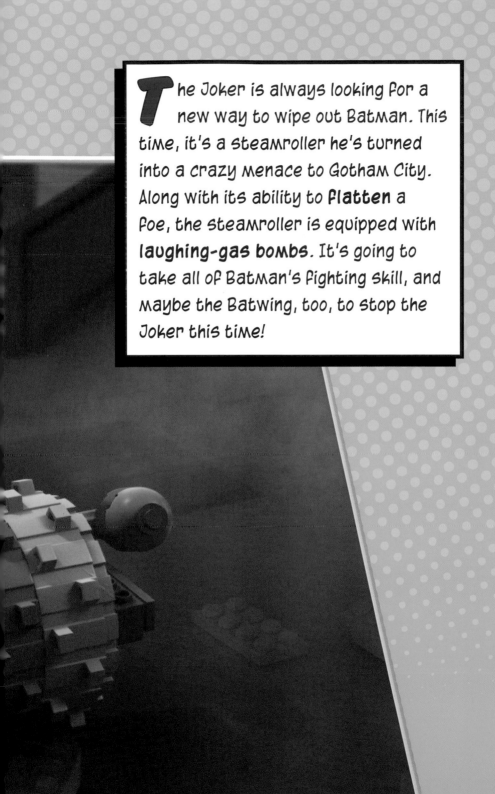

The Joker is always looking for a new way to wipe out Batman. This time, it's a steamroller he's turned into a crazy menace to Gotham City. Along with its ability to **flatten** a foe, the steamroller is equipped with **laughing-gas bombs**. It's going to take all of Batman's fighting skill, and maybe the Batwing, too, to stop the Joker this time!

HAWKMAN'S SHIP

When his wings are not enough, Hawkman takes to the skies with his **ship**. Fast and highly **manoeuvrable**, Hawkman relies on it to stay one step ahead of **super-villains**. Whether in the air or outer space, nowhere above ground is safe for super-villains to hide!

CHAPTER 4
LOCATIONS!

THE LEGO DC UNIVERSE IS FILLED WITH PLACES THAT ARE EXCITING, MYSTERIOUS AND DANGEROUS. IN ANY CORNER OF THE WORLD, YOU MIGHT FIND A SUPER HERO'S SECRET BASE OR THE HIDDEN HIDEOUT OF A MASTER VILLAIN. ALTHOUGH A HERO OR VILLAIN MIGHT BE NORMALLY SEEN IN ONE CITY, THEY OFTEN TRAVEL ELSEWHERE. SO DON'T BE SURPRISED TO SEE WONDER WOMAN IN METROPOLIS OR AQUAMAN IN GOTHAM CITY!

GOTHAM CITY

Gotham City is the home city of **Batman** and **Robin**. It is also home to a number of super-villains and a lot of **crime**, so Batman is always busy. Gotham City was, at one time, a thriving place, but it has fallen on hard times. That is why there are so many abandoned factories and warehouses for super-villains to use as **hideouts**.

Some of the famous sites in Gotham City include the Wayne Enterprises building, Robinson Park, Gotham Heights, Wayne Manor, Gotham Stadium and Arkham Asylum.

METROPOLIS

Metropolis is one of the largest and most famous cities in the DC Universe, because it is the home of **Superman**. Metropolis is a much more **modern** city than Gotham City, with glass-and-steel skyscrapers everywhere as well as the Daily Planet Building. Superman works for the *Daily Planet* in his other identity of Clark Kent.

Metropolis sees its share of action, with **alien invaders** and super-villains often showing up there to take on the Man of Steel. Fortunately, Superman is able to rapidly repair any damage done to the city by his battles.

THE BATCAVE

Batman and Robin's **secret headquarters**, the Batcave, is located beneath Wayne Manor in Gotham City. Batman has filled it with everything he needs for his fight against crime, from the **Batcomputer** to a special elevator for costume changes and a **holding cell** for dangerous prisoners like Poison Ivy. Batman also keeps his awesome vehicles here, including the Batcycle. The location of the Batcave is a closely guarded secret, but at least one Batman villain — Bane — has found it in the past.

The *Daily Planet* is the biggest and most successful newspaper in Metropolis. Superman works there in his identity as **Clark Kent,** alongside **Lois Lane.** The *Daily Planet* has broken many major news stories, and been the site of battles between Superman and arch-foes, alien invaders and cosmic monsters. The Daily Planet Building is famous for the giant **globe** on its roof.

LEXCORP

LexCorp is one of the world's biggest conglomerates, owned and operated by Lex Luthor. It is headquartered in Metropolis, but has offices all over the world. Its research **labs** produce many of the weapons used by Luthor against Superman, as well as doing studies on **Kryptonite**. Despite Luthor's many crimes, no one has been able to shut LexCorp down yet.

THE HALL OF JUSTICE

This is the famous headquarters of the Justice League. From here, the super heroes monitor the planet with the **Trouble Alert**, ever on the watch for dangers. Other features of the Hall include a conference room, laboratory, jail cell, living quarters, kitchen, teleportation units, computer centre and more. One Justice League member must be on monitor duty at the Hall at all times.

LOST TEMPLE OF POSEIDON

Far beneath the surface of the ocean is the legendary Temple of Poseidon, its location long forgotten by ancient **Atlanteans**. Black Manta travels here to attempt to steal the **Trident of Poseidon**, but he's opposed by Batman and Aquaman. When Black Manta finally gets his hands on the trident, the temple comes crashing down around him. The ancient site is lost forever now.

BIZARRO WORLD

Bizarro World is a strange, square-shaped planet that is home to Bizarro Superman and various other Bizarros. Its capital city is **Bizarrotropolis**, a twisted version of Metropolis. On Bizarro World, everything is done the opposite of how it's done on Earth. Bizarro World is protected by the Bizarro League, imperfect copies of the Justice League members.

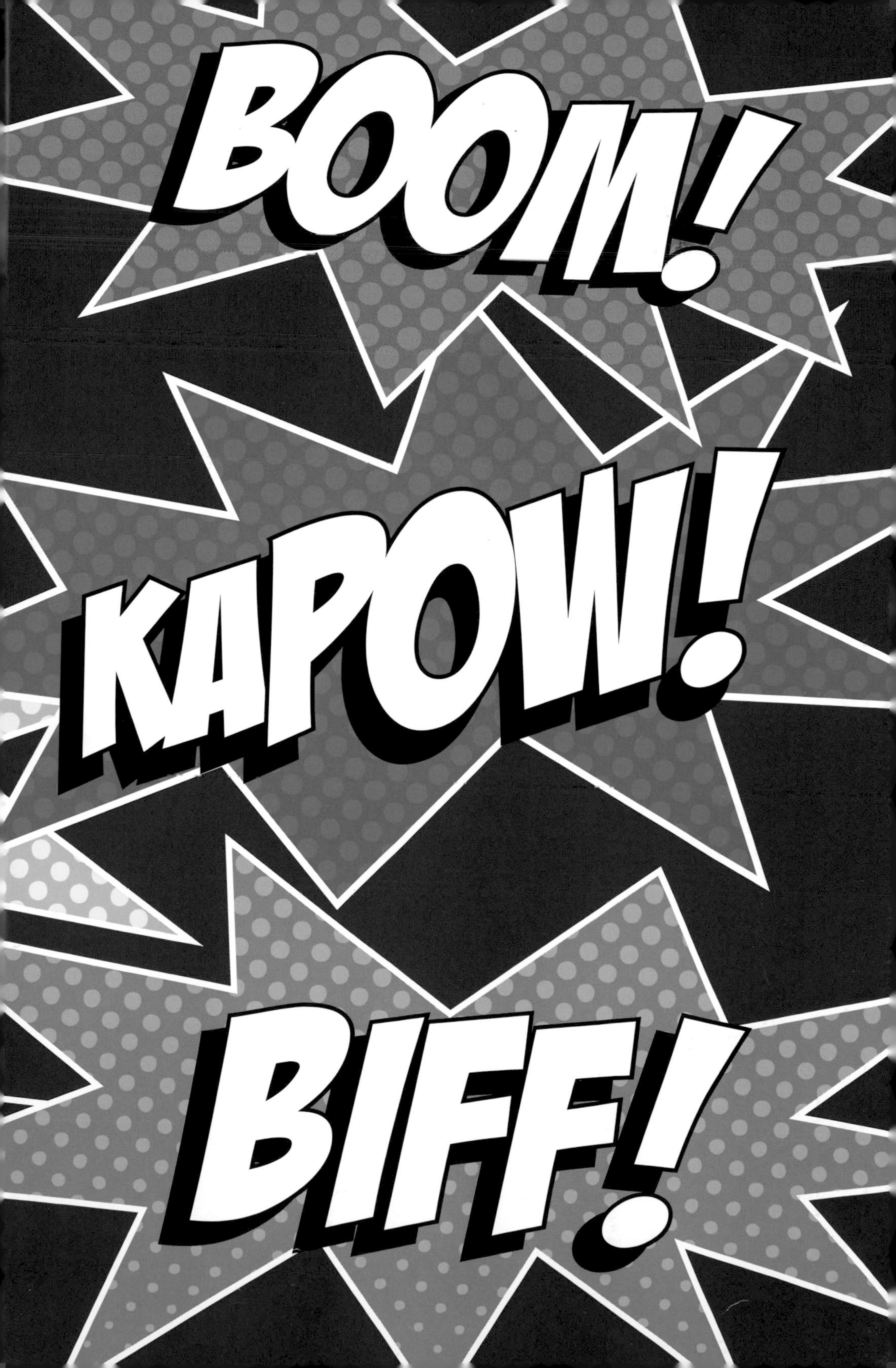
BOOM!
KAPOW!
BIFF!